HOW ANYONE CAN BECOME A
MESSENGER FROM SPIRIT... HELPING
OTHERS & YOURSELF!

The Only Instruction
You Need To Reignite Your Natural
Inborn Ability!

MEDIUMSHIP

BY IDA PIMM

ADAPTED BY JOHN RICHARDSON

Matador
9 Priory Business Park,
Wistow Road, Kibworth Beauchamp,
Leicestershire. LE8 0RX
Tel: 0116 279 2299
Email: books@troubador.co.uk
Web: www.troubador.co.uk/matador
Twitter: @matadorbooks

ISBN 978 1838591 168

British Library Cataloguing in Publication Data.
A catalogue record for this book is available from the British Library.

Typeset in 11pt Minion Pro by Troubador Publishing Ltd, Leicester, UK

Matador is an imprint of Troubador Publishing Ltd

This book is dedicated to my Granny-May.
It is not academic because neither was she.
It is not prodigious... but just enough.

Ida Pimm
'Revealing the truth about Mediumship'

'In this book you will find no contents,
because sometimes in life it's best not to know
what's coming next'

– Ida Pimm

Foreword

THIS BOOK IS FOCUSED ON a dedicated readership. There are many thousands of individuals who continue to practice psychic and mediumistic doctrines. Contrary to belief spiritualism is not on the decline. Many people in their early twenties have an interest in the subject. Therefore the breadth of the age of the readers is significant (late teens to octogenarians). Not only this, the fascination is worldwide.

One issue is the 'spiritual churches' have failed to keep up with modern demands of time and accessibility. People lead lives with different timetables: Inevitably, many of the older spiritualist churches have now closed their doors. The closures have led to a high demand for teachings from new sources.

Teaching the methods of psychic and mediumistic work has become a thriving industry. The difficulty is many of the 'teachers' have no practical experience, and many of the courses offered fall well short of the mark. Very few fulfil the claims of the prospectus. Although, on the contrary, there are some very good ones too: So do your homework first before you sign on the dotted line!

John Richardson is fortunate to be a member of a family with a long and verifiable history as psychics and spiritual mediums. Due to this 'connection', he has built an excellent reputation in this field. His opinion carries influence with those connected to, and interested in, the world of spiritualism. Some time ago he was presented with a short manuscript written by his aunt, found in a drawer shortly after her death. Her name was Ida Pimm. As John read through Ida's work, he realised its content would appeal to a vast audience.

There is a shortage of 'hands-on' information about the world of spirit. This book fulfils the demands of thousands who wish to learn about the traditional methods of spiritualism. One of the most appealing aspects of the book is Ida's words can be used effectively by the lone investigator. By studying the 'body' of the work, they can develop their psychic and mediumistic abilities: Probably the only instruction they will ever need.

The book is worthy and will be useful for all those who have an interest in spiritual awareness and development. It is straightforward to read and easy to understand. There are few (if any) books on this subject written by an authentic, established medium. Ida practised mediumship for over sixty years, something which the reader of this subject will find of immense appeal.

Another appealing aspect for readers of the genre is John Richardson's reputation as a psychic and spiritual medium. I have known John for many years, both professionally and as a personal friend – Training and studying hypnosis at the same school of thought, and I know people will choose this book based on John's status: Especially amongst his loyal and dedicated following. I feel this book will enjoy a demand for many years in the future: Providing the key for many to the spirit world.

The book provides a rare insight into the methodology of a renowned psychic/medium. Ida's methods are revealed in the body of the book: It is easy to follow for the reader/ student and while admittedly specialist, the demand for this type of writing is consistent with a loyal reader base and the quest for spiritual enlightenment: So read and learn!

Eb Black – Holistic (Spiritual) Hypnotherapist
USA

Preface

WHEN JOHN ASKED ME TO read through the original manuscript of 'Ida Pimm' I had no idea what to expect. As I read past his introduction, I soon realised this is a unique, exciting book.

John had the manuscript 'proofread' although he warned me his instructions to the proofreader was to keep the essence of the work untouched. As you read through the book take your time. Remember, Ida's words are as she put them to paper. I like the 'feel' of the writing: Once past the first few paragraphs, there is a real connection to this insightful lady.

For anyone who has an interest in 'mediumistic' work, this book is a treasure trove of information. Ida takes the reader on a journey of exploration and learning. From my perspective, the simplicity of the lessons have more impact than the complex explanation of the spirit world, and it's inhabitants provided by other authors.

Of course, there will be information the reader will already know. And there will be areas which may not fit with present practices. Don't let this stop you from testing Ida's teaching: The probability is, there is much to be learned from her years of mediumistic experience.

Many of us remember the 'old school' mediums of childhood. How different the world is today. The old ways are most often lost forever, so it is excellent that Ida chose to write about her work and methods. There is much to learn from this short manuscript.

It is evident she loved her work and connecting to the 'spirit world'. Her message is the spirit world is a safe place to connect to and enjoy. There is a reference to imagined dangers. She writes; people's fears are manifest by inaccurate thoughts; often instilled by the imagination of the ignorant. Ida writes about certain methods of protection from 'misguided spirits'. Interestingly she writes about how to protect from the negative influence of living people. Do not be surprised if you begin to like Ida very much indeed.

I wondered how long Ida took to write the teachings and I asked about her voice and home. During a conversation with John, he told me about her home and the way she lived. It seemed strange that he confirmed the images formed in my mind as I read the pages. Is it possible her spirit connected to me during my reading of her words?

This is a great book. Yes! It takes a little time to follow and all credit to John for keeping the words as original as possible. Honing every sentence and paragraph would lose the essence of Ida's teaching.

I'm confident those who seek information about the 'spirit world' will find this book of great interest. With this in mind: We must thank John Richardson for taking the time and spending the money to make this book available. I'm sure you'll enjoy meeting Ida. I know my time with her was fascinating.

Ian Timothy – April 2019

Introduction By
John Richardson

PEOPLE ASK, AM I A Medium? Growing up I had the privilege of not only having a grandfather who was a medium but also an aunt too: She was Ida Pimm. Ida was my grandfather's cousin and although technically auntie may not have been her correct prefix, and should have been my first cousin twice removed. During my childhood auntie seemed an easier way to address her: So, auntie, it was. Both auntie Ida and my grandfather nurtured me through my formative years and taught me how to keep connected to my Natural Inborn Abilities. I will be forever grateful to these two extraordinary people for making me always aware of my spiritual being and making my childhood one of a spiritual nature. Looking back at my childhood I always knew I was a little different than all the other children, which I managed to prove many times over, and not always in a good way, as bullying often accompanies being different, but without auntie Ida and my grandfather I may have always thought I was different without knowing the real reason why – I now see it as what doesn't kill you makes you stronger and the material that built the foundations of the person I have now become. I was fortunate to have these mentors: It is my belief that their ability to guide me through my doubts and fears helped me keep my innate mediumship ability alive. Many young people close the 'gates of insight' as they grow into adolescence and once closed only a few manage to re-enter the 'gardens of wisdom' as an adult.

Helping people find closure and direction in their lives is something extraordinary and highly rewarding, and I have never wished to walk any other path than the one I feel was chosen for me. I know I was born lucky having the good fortune of spending countless numbers of hours in the company of auntie Ida and my grandfather who became more than just family but also my teachers and mentors as my mediumship developed with age: And with the help of this book, I feel they can become yours too. Looking back I now know that I was being, may I say, covertly nurtured in preparation for when I would take my rightful place in the lineage of my family mediums. I know they both knew the path I would eventually take even though at that time I was very much unaware of what would subsequently lie before me. At times I also resisted, but I feel this was the immature child in me stamping his feet. I could not have asked for two better teachers as being of the same blood everything was done with my best interest at heart.

With time my grandfather would also pass on to me his skills as a hypnotist which has provided me with a very successful career and the two, hypnosis and mediumship, blended gave me my unique style of hypnotherapy that had produced many outstanding results even when everything else had failed. I still cannot understand why the two, hypnosis and mediumship, are mostly kept poles apart in many schools of thought when the only benefit of their mix is one of great success and advantage. There are still so many times when I think to myself of how many questions I wish I had have asked, but at the time I did not realise the value of the knowledge stored within these two very extraordinary people.

When my auntie passed over to the spirit world, and her family had emptied her house, notes were found written in a journal containing instruction on mediumship and spiritual development that she had written at various times in her life. These notes were passed on to me as her children thought that this is what she would have wanted. With the consent of her family, I've decided to put her writings into a book; exactly as initially penned. They are in her own words with even her quirky punctuation staying the same, you know, the odd straying comer and misplaced capital letter: Although I had a few blanks to fill, hopefully to her satisfaction. As I read the words you will be reading soon I can still hear her voice filling each word with wisdom and knowledge, and I know she will be so glad to be, now, of service to you. The simplicity of her language will make for natural learning for the aspiring medium and exciting reading for the curious mind. I had the privilege of growing up with this amazing lady, and at the end of these words, I feel you too will come to know and love my auntie, Ida Pimm, as much as I do.

Read on and take all you need to reconnect your 'Natural Inborn Abilities'. Whether to help others or yourself. By the end of this book, I'm hoping auntie Ida becomes as much your muse as mine. And the answer to the question, am I a Medium, of course you are!

John Richardson – February 2019

Granny-May

Ida Pimm

J. Arthur Laundon

John Richardson

How My Journey Began

Ida Pimm

I WAS NOT BROUGHT UP IN a spiritual family, well, not in the type we are going to talk about here. As a child, we regularly attended our village church on a Sunday morning for holy communion, but to me, this was just someone telling me what to do, especially the long and challenging sermons I had to endure: Bossy! Unaware to me at this time my grandmother (Granny-May) was working as an 'underground' medium and healer from her little rose-covered cottage two miles from our home in the country. This sounds a bit funny at the time of writing these words as today mediumship has become generally excepted and visiting a medium, and having a reading, is something now recognised as an entirely reasonable thing to do: But not back then hence, Granny-May, the underground medium.

When my grandmother was working, she would have been treated more like a witch and very different to that of the blatantly open mediums of today: That is if she had ever been exposed. Where today you will see mediums on TV performing their Natural Inborn Abilities without even the raising of a brow, something my grandmother would have loved to have done, though, would have probably ended up on the ducking-stool if she had made her mediumship abilities known and performed them publicly: And TV would have been impossible as yet still to be invented: Or at best made popular.

I used to visit my grandmother on Sunday afternoons after church with my mother, father and younger brother. We would stay for tea then walk the two miles back home often in the dark. Even though I knew nothing of my grandmothers mediumship, she was something of an oddity, excitingly. She had a budgie next to her chair that talked with a higher vocabulary than most academics and a spaniel that would curl lovingly around her feet. Her home smelt of herbs and baking. It had fantastic energy which could be felt on entering that made you want to stay and never leave. Her dulcet tones would melt the coldest of hearts, and you never saw her without a smile, and as she would say, a smile costs nothing. Her husband, my grandfather, had passed to the other side of life two years before me being born but she always talked about him, and to him, as though he was still in the room and now knowing what I know he mostly was. She used to say, Your granddad loves you very much and is watching over you: He will always keep you safe. I feel she knew at that time I would be working with spirit one-day, of which I knew nothing.

I stayed at my grandmothers as often as possible. She would make me a tent with the clotheshorse, and an old blanket and all my meals would be taken into the tent and often she would join me: Such fun. I would often feel sorry for her living alone, but with age, I became acutely aware of the many people that visited her home, but for some reason, at that time I never asked why. When someone came I was told to play silently while she would take the visitor through into her front room, always referred to as the best room, then after an hour or so they would appear with happy tears, and a beaming smile or someone would arrive with crutches and leave shortly after with them under their arm. But nothing was ever mentioned about the visits, and as mentioned earlier my curiosity never made me ask why: It was just what she did and I knew no different. I am even quite sure her daughter, my mother, was unaware of her readings, healing's and her spiritual work because she never spoke anything of it. I felt very close to my grandmother and an exceptional relationship would evolve as my years advanced.

One summer in my thirteenth year I was staying at my grandmothers for a full week in the school summer holidays: Yea! I hadn't been there more than half a day when she said she wanted to talk, but it was something she wanted to keep between just us two. This felt very special to me. After putting a meat and potato pie and

Bramley apple pie (All the leftover pastry was placed into the bottom of the oven and baked hence the name 'oven bottom cake' then eaten with treacle... yum-yum) into the oven we went into the 'best room' with freshly made lemonade and a ginger-nut each that my grandmother had made that morning, and we sat on two chairs each side of what she calls her gipsy table: And the conversation went something like this.

She started by saying, you know the friends you played with when you were little, well, these were spirit children that only you and I could see. I replied by saying that they never came anymore. Grandma told me that they did. But, as we get older, our minds become full of other things that we stop seeing them: The loss of 'purity of mind'. You are an extraordinary girl Ida because you are a sensitive Soul and you can talk to these spirits again if you want to. "Oh! Yes, grandma, I want to". I exclaimed. She told me to imagine a tall tower that vanished high into the clouds. This is your tower of consciousness she said. The majority of people live all their life on the ground floor of their tower but if you wish you can take the elevator to your highest floors of consciousness at will: With a little practice.

That means going to any higher level of your knowledge whenever you want to, intending to enrich your life and the lives of others by more extensive and efficient use of your mind and its innate psychic power. Your childhood spirit friends will be on the third floor waiting for you, and once you learn how to take the elevator to the third floor (meditation/self-hypnosis), you will meet them again. The third floor is called 'Theta' or 'The Theta-State', and this is the state-of-consciousness where we can reignite our Natural Inborn Ability and launch into the psychic experience. And to reach the third floor, we need to meditate and lots of it. There is no limit to how high the elevator can take you, but for now lets enjoy our lemonade and ginger nut and remember, said grandma, this is our little secret, something that seems so wrong as I write these words but looking back it was so right as the majority of people would never have understood at the time, my parents included.

Unaware to me my cousin Arthur was going through the same spiritual nurturing as myself but Granny-May would keep our journey's separate because as she explained in later years, spiritual development is a very personal journey: As we all develop at a different pace. Arthur became a popular Medium, Healer and Hypnotist / Hypnotherapist in his home village and as cousins, we would play together not knowing of each other's spiritual journeys.

How strange. In our adult life, we worked together a lot and spent hours comparing notes and talking all things spiritual: Apart from being cousins we became great friends and shared the love of Granny-May. I recall her telling Arthur that he will have a grandson that will follow in both our footsteps and will have the benefit of both our nurturing as you have mine.

From that day on my journey started. The reason for writing these words is to allow people to live the life I have led in the company of Spirit thanks to my grandmother, but only if you want to as Spirit will never go where they are not wanted! I want to help you reconnect with your Natural Inborn Abilities. I don't like the word gift because it makes it sound unique to the person who receives the gift, and it's not: The gift is our degree of sensitivity. We are all born with mediumship abilities. Some temporary stop using them for a multitude of reasons and never regain them, while others do. If a telephone line gets cut, it needs mending before you can reconnect and communicate once more. My grandmother taught me how to reconnect my telephone line to the Spirit World, and I would like to pass her knowledge on to you. I'm not saying that everyone will be a fantastic medium, hence the degree of sensitivity we are blessed with, but everybody can achieve some degree of mediumship, and with practice, we can all improve. It is a simple process and not something that should be made difficult and over protracted to justify the often large sums of money that change hands for the privilege of the teaching and training thought needed: It's about rediscovering not creating!

Trust me this is not necessary as most development can be done in the company of oneself and free of charge. All you need is a few simple instructions and a little guidance, and that is what I aim to do for you. So if you ask the question; Am I a Medium. Then the answer is a simple YES! You see everyone can play the piano if they want, but some can play it better than others depending on dedication and practice. Once a lady asked me to show her how she could connect to Spirit. I told her she would need to meditate and I would teach her how. Right now. I guided her through fifteen minutes of meditation but all through I could hear her fidgeting. Amazingly, she did manage to complete the reflection, but the first thing she asked upon opening her eyes was how long had it taken. I told her fifteen minutes, saying that I used to meditate for an hour in the morning and evening in my early years of development. She said that she could never manage that long and I said; "Then you will never be as good as me: But you can be... All depending on dedication and commitment!"

So let start at the beginning:

Well, it is a very good place to start. Using mediumistic skills is nothing new; in fact, it is as old as time itself. It is something we are all born with and lost and not some new age discovery. In centuries past everyone did it from the Incas to the Egyptians – The Native American Indians to the Maya's. The Shaman relayed heavily on the knowledge of their ancestors and was in constant communication daily. It was a regular part of everyday life. How nice it must have been not having the thought that your loved-ones leave you at death and always knowing they are forever around you, forever passing on their wisdom. It would make me very sad to think that on death all our knowledge is lost, well it's not, and if we all listen we could learn a lot from our ancestors still to this day. It's the material things that are valueless as upon our move to the other side of life the only thing we can take with us is our experiences... thoughts, memories, knowledge... the contents of our mind (You won't need Pickford's for that).

The man who strives for material wealth has nothing of any value, but the man who strives for Spiritual

Enlightenment has everything. He is a very wealthy man, and his wealth cannot be stolen, so neither has he any fear of loss: Money is only as good as the experiences it buys! My grandmother always said that worrying about material loss is a fools greatest fear. You see when we understand that we never die, everything we accumulate in mind we keep forever, but the physical is only temporary, and of no great long-term value, then we come to see the bigger picture. The physical human body is nothing more than a vehicle for the Soul. Without it we are no different, just less visible to the human eye: But is this because we are just not looking hard enough as we expect everything in this world to be of a tangible nature? So the first belief that most people need to change when finding and reigniting their Natural Inborn Abilities is that on death no-one goes anywhere they are still here, just like you and me, though now less visible, but can contact and be contacted for all eternity. Isn't that a great thought? Just knowing we are never alone. This is one of my greatest truths as I always feared loneliness and by finding Spirit again quashed all my fears. The physical human body has an expiry date just like a car has a limited life but when a vehicle breaks we get a new one and maybe for a short period we have to live without one. When we scrap a car we don't stay inside it, we climb out. Our bodies are no different.

Everyone can use their Natural Inborn Abilities, often called their sixth sense. Some rediscover it and choose to use it, while others never find it again because they choose not to. If you read the words I am putting on this paper then you, whoever you are, can reignite your Natural

Inborn Abilities and talk to Spirit once more. And that is my promise to you. I can remember my grandmother showing me how to protect myself and how to connect to Spirit, of which all this is to come shortly... Patience my dear... And then she just threw a pack of cards at me and said; Now read for me! I must admit it was a bit sketchy, but I did get something although at this time my diction was a bit limited. But how simple is that... And it is that simple. But the three main words you will have to learn is Trust, Respect and Gratitude (TRG) and these three simple words are the magic key to your degree of success! And my philosophy is always, 'KEEP IT SIMPLE', because it's not as difficult as people often lead you to believe, usually only to make themselves feel special and ego feeding.

So I am presuming by reading this book you are now ready to reignite your 'Natural Inborn Abilities' or at least hold some curiosity about the subject. You may even be new to this or may have been trying for a while, but wherever you are on your journey, I am sure this book will help and guide you further along your spiritual path. You may even amaze yourself at what you can achieve. I aim to show you in a no-nonsense, quick and easy way how to connect to the Spirit world which is also one hundred percent safe at all times. In all my years of working with Spirit, and there have been many, I have never once encountered anything that has frightened me or caused me a problem. Remember: I have always worked through love and light and always for benefit of my fellow man: Trust me it is nothing like the films of Boris Karloff, Vincent Price and Peter Cushing. Thank God. So now you know a little about me lets get on with the job of making you the medium you always were!

So let us make a start:

Excited? Well, you should be because this is the most magnificent journey you will ever take: The Orient Express is nothing compared to this! I am going to show you a safe and effective way of reconnecting your Natural Inborn Abilities. A lot of people start with circles at spiritual churches or in private homes. Unless these circles are run with an iron fist by an experienced medium who is very aware of human nature, then ego can stop the development of many would be mediums: And that is such a shame.

As stated earlier the medium is a sensitive and as a sensitive words and actions can cut very deep so unless the medium running the circle is a nurturer, and keen observer, development in a circle, can be hindered or halted by another person's actions or words. If you are one of the lucky ones and drop on the right circle then this can be a fantastic experience, and you can indeed develop very quickly because the energy a circle creates is second to none and the available knowledge to be drawn upon can be your library, but often the flaw can be other members egos and, or, issues. So I always recommend obtaining a level of knowledge and a little experience first, then do your homework and find the right circle for you if that's the path you want to take. But circles are not for everyone and definitely not mandatory to success.

Another potential problem with circles, or indeed groups of people who meet regularly, is that we can learn a lot about each other from overhearing conversations, say over the mandatory coffee break, then using that information to feed ego in the messages they give. That I feel is why some people never leave the safety of the circle and give messages or read for Joe Public. But always remember mediumship is not all about reading and delivering messages to others, it also about using it for yourself to make better decisions from receiving guidance from the Divine, your Guides and your Spirit family: This is probably the first in importance! So reading for others is secondary to reading (spiritual contact) for yourself. We read for others because we want to and enjoy to, but fundamentally mediumship is for you! Human nature is extraordinary because, on the one hand, the seed of all humanity is love and light but often life experiences can produce a distorted perspective of life, and there will be a percentage of people that don't want you to be seen as exceeding their own capabilities for whatever reasons they hold: Teachers, mentors, leaders included!

Choose your instructors carefully! When working with Spirit life balance is very important. Keep time for your spiritual work and a time for the physicality's of life, or just don't become obsessed and let your mediumship occupy all of your time. There is a time for both: You are not a monk (or nun). And we are put here to experience life in all its dimensions: Exploring and learning from all its aspects. So have a go at everything. Although I'm not sure about Morris-dancing!

For a person to be a medium, they have to have some degree of awareness. To enable them to feel that they have someone there with them or around them. A lot of practising mediums have many stories to tell of strange and unexplained experiences in childhood (spirit friends, etc.), and never really feeling alone when the house is empty or when somewhere by themselves: They are very sensitive. This awareness is created or enhanced by meditation, or you could say cultivated through development.

Most mediums have walked difficult pathways due to their sensitivity, for example, you could say to one person my dog has died this morning, and that person would reply, Oh dear, I am sorry, then carry on with their day as though nothing had happened, never giving it a second thought. Then another person would respond to the same scenario with, are you alright, I feel your pain. Often been affected for the rest of the day, or two, or more. The second would develop the easiest with the first probably never even considering it. So if you are drawn to mediumship, then its most likely you are a 'sensitive' anyway. Do you watch a film (even a cartoon) and if it has a sad ending do you think about it after the credits have rolled? I have all my films vetted before I watch them as their effects were so bad I could feel them for weeks after. Arthur, my cousin, once explained that the subconscious part of our mind cannot tell the difference between something imagined and something real and will respond equally the same to both. So if you are a Highly Sensitive Person (HSP) these effects can be very emotive for days, even weeks after the film has ended. Granny-May would often say that sensitivity is a blessing and a curse but to be a medium you need it, and she would not want to be without it, as the rewards from mediumship are so high. "You have to come to understand it" she would say. And it doesn't stop when you start working for Spirit or use Spirit in your own life, in fact, it can even get a little more testing (brace yourself, but don't let it put you off) as more things can be thrown at you to test you further for personal growth and advancement. But Granny-May said that Spirit would never give you more than you can bear and just because you are a sensitive doesn't mean you are weak and vulnerable. You may have just come to believe that you are weak because you are emotive.

But the contrary is true, Highly Sensitive People are the most resilient personality types of all and hold great strength, they have to be, they often carry everyone else's problems, in their minds. One of the things I stopped doing was listening to the news because it had disastrous effects on my daily life. So I now follow the rule of 'change the things you can change but don't worry about the things you can't', and this has served me well. If I could change the world I would, I can't, but I can change a little in my village, and I do, what I can. Don't let this put you off because working with Spirit will be one of the most rewarding things you can do and I wouldn't change a thing: When you connect two souls, one in Spirit and one on earth; there is no greater reward known to man. Thank you Granny-May!

You don't need to understand what the spirit world is like to be able to communicate with Spirit. There are thousands of accounts of what the spirit world is like with some claiming to have even visited. If you become one of the lucky ones to have this experience you too will be able to document your experience but right now I feel it is not essential.

All you have to know is that Spirit communicates through thought, or Mind to Mind. Intuition is your inner-voice and the primary way I receive my messages. Some say what can you hear, and the only answer I can give is, an inner-voice without a noise: You will come to understand and need to know that whatever your intuition tells you will be correct and you have to learn to trust. The more you work with Spirit, the more your awareness will grow and expand. So right now don't be too hard on yourself or expect too much. The key to the spirit world is our imagination and Spirit impress thoughts upon us whether an image (Clairvoyance), a voice (Clairaudience), a feeling (Clairsentience), pure knowing (Claircognisance) and so on. So when someone says they see Spirit, it is usually within their mind. Spirit can and often do appear under various circumstances. But the effort is so great. Typically, the image is in the mind of the medium. Remember, everything starts as a thought. The mind is a receiver and will pick up information from other minds whether in body or spirit. Spirit communication is a form of telepathy. Spirit talk to each other not by mouth but in their mind and that is also how they speak to us: Mind To Mind. We have to learn a whole new language, the universal language of the Spirit world. Don't worry: It's so much easier than French or German.

So now let's do a little exercise with your imagination. Close your eyes and I would like you to imagine someone you know who has passed over to the other side of life standing in front of you. Imagine the detail in their face. Imagine: What clothes are they wearing. Imagine: What are their shoes like, dull or shiny. Imagine: Do they have any unusual characteristics. Spend a few moments now creating as much detail as possible. Don't force it. Just let it happen. Ask the person a question and see if they give you an answer or ask if they have a message for you? When you are ready slowly open your eyes and return to the here and now.

Did you find this exercise easy or hard? If you found it hard at your first attempt, I promise it will become more comfortable each time you practice it. So practice! When learning to ride a bike, we often fall off. If we don't jump right back on, we will never learn to ride as practice makes perfect. As children, our imaginations run wild. We use it all the time when we play because when we play, we imagine. As we get older, we use the gift less, and it becomes lost: Some people forget how to use it at all. Often people think it infantile to imagine and play, but it is a great escape and a short break from reality. It always makes me laugh when grown-ups become collectors of toys and dolls because I bet that when no-one is looking that little toy tractor comes out with all the engine noises being made by the collector or the doll needs feeding when no-one is home but you.

TRY THIS EXPERIMENT OF ASSOCIATION:

Imagine you're holding a fresh lemon.
Smell it: What does it smell like?
Feel It: What does it feel like?

Imagine putting the lemon on a table and taking a knife you cut the lemon in half. See the tangy juice run from the lemon. Now pick up one half and lick it. Keep your tongue on the lemon and if you dare suck it. Is your mouth watering yet? Is it making you screw your face up? Maybe your eyes are watering? It is probable this exercise proves your mind cannot tell the difference between something imagined and something real.

Remember imagination is the key to the spirit world, and like anything the more we use it, the better we get; but we do need to persist. Development takes time, you cannot rush it, and you will develop in whatever time is right for you. If you get knocked down then get right back up. Because staying down is nothing more than wasting valuable development time and slowing the whole process down. And I never once want to hear the word can't because if I can then so can you. Consider yourself told.

Most mediums see Spirit this way. In their mind. We have to tune into their channel, and we do this by stilling the mind. I cannot overemphasise how important meditation is to your development. We have to learn that when we are working with Spirit, we have to return back to our pure state of mind: Free from pollution and without distortion.

We have to train the mind to calm-down on cue or achieve an altered state of consciousness, and with time and practice, this becomes an automatic process. I use a switch in my mind. The switch says at the top 'Ida' and at the bottom 'Spiritual Ida', and I switch accordingly when working and when not. The switch came about when I said to Granny-May that I was constantly bombarded with voices. Oh! My dear, she would say, its only because you are new and all your Spirit friends want to chat to you. You are so popular: The switch did the trick.

Spirit now know when I'm working and when I've clocked off. The only time they come through when I am not working is if something important needs to be said to me or to someone I am to come across that day. And that's just fine. Once again I cannot overemphasise the importance of meditation. Meditation puts you in an altered state of consciousness where we close down the outside physical world for a while and opening up the inside world of Spirit and self-awareness. Haven't you noticed that usually when people see Spirit, it's just before falling asleep or only upon awakening? Once we regain full consciousness, the Spirit disappears. The Spirit is still there; it's just the junk in your mind, made conscious, obscures your view.

Also when we are asleep Spirit find it very easy to communicate with us and this is often the time when we get prophetic dreams and Spirit communication, and we think we are just dreaming. In all my years of working with Spirit, I have never experienced anything unpleasant or in the least bit frightening. I often joke with my sitters that if a ghost appears then its every-man for themselves. If you ask to see Spirit, I am sure at some point you will see Spirit, but I am just fine the way it is. Thank you very much. I only ever work with love and light and ask for only information that is loving and purposeful, and that is precisely what I get: The dark side is not for me. I am not that brave. Spirit respect the nature of everyone of us so we all get what we can deal with and nothing more.

Meditation should be done regularly! Start with short periods of five minutes in the morning and the same again in the evening; increasing with time and practice. If at the beginning you start with meditations that are too long you will tire, become frustrated, and probably quit. Meditation should be an enjoyable experience so start small. I began with candle gazing. That's watching a candle flame, concentrating on the flame. Then if my mind wandered gently letting go of the intruding thought and bring my attention back to the flame. You can do this with crystals, pictures, in-fact anything of your choice. Also guided meditations are good for the busy and active minds as they keep you focused on the next instruction.

Remember, meditation is not sleeping. If you go to sleep you are not meditating you are asleep. That's why it is not right to contemplate in bed when you are tired as the bed is a sign to your subconscious mind that its time for sleep... And that's often what happens when you try to meditate in bed. Sat on a straight back chair with your feet planted firmly on the floor is often the best way to meditate and don't be too hard on yourself at first. Routine is best as anything repeated over and over again becomes a habit and second nature so try and meditate at the same times each day. We aim to settle and still the mind to clear the way for spiritual communication.

My cousin Arthur used self-hypnosis techniques, so there are many avenues for you to explore to find the right method for you to heighten your awareness to all things spiritual. But remember your development will take time. There was a story I was once told about a young Monk who was meditating under a great oak tree. He had been contemplating for one year when a traveller passing by and seeing the Monk asked: "Hows the meditation going?" The Monk replied: "Whatever I do I cannot empty my mind". The traveller seeing the young Monk was disappointed said: "If you go up high into the mountains there you will find a Monk who has been meditating for fifty years, and I am sure he will show you how to empty your mind. If anyone can, he can". So the young Monk stood up and instantly set off in search of his answer. As he climbed higher and higher into the mountains he saw in front of him an elderly Monk sat cross-legged perched right at the top of one of the mountain peaks. He walked up to him and tugged on his robes and said: "Please can you help me?" "I have been meditating for one full year now, and I cannot empty my mind no matter how hard I try".

The old Monk turned slowly and said: "No, neither can I". We cannot empty the mind totally, but neither is that the objective of meditation. Our aim is to train the mind to still and concentrate on the moment, so it is open for communication and not obscured and distracted with other things of lesser importance. When meditating and a rogue thought enters your mind just let it go. Don't analyse the idea: Only return to the focal point of your meditation. With TIME and PRACTISE the intruding thoughts in your meditations will become less and less.

When working with Spirit your mind becomes focused on the NOW: Not the FUTURE or the PAST –

Listening to Spirit. This is how we grow, raise and expand our awareness. We also contact, communicate and build relationships with our Guides and Spirit family through meditation: More on Guides and Spirit family later; but for now get meditating and start your journey to Spiritual awareness on your voyage of inner discovery.

Let's talk now about protection and grounding. As our awareness grows and expands we become more sensitive to all the energies around us. We have to protect ourselves, so we are not carrying any unnecessary baggage that doesn't belong to us. It's like shutting your front door when visitors leave and making sure they take all they brought with them: And nothing of yours. When you start working with your Guides and your Spirit family you will be able to ask them to take things away, like, often if a Spirit has had a bad back in this life, or some other pains, they will make me feel them in the places where they had them so I can validate with the sitter that this person is the person who they say they are, and this is the proof needed by the sitter. It is the message which also becomes the evidence of the connection. Sometimes they may leave the pain a little too long, so I ask my Guides to 'tell' them to take it away: Though this is rare.

When we choose to work with Spirit: We can become aware of the atmosphere in a room where an argument has taken place. Or we can take an instant dislike or like to a particular person before words are exchanged. This is because we are sensitive, often feeling things others wouldn't. So we have to protect this sensitivity. Once we realise that we and everyone else is made of energy, and another energy can have an effect on us, then we understand how vital it is to understand grounding and protection. Once protection and grounding become a part of your morning routine within a few days you will notice a difference. You may feel less tired, drained and emotionally negative. A noticeable increase in physical and mental energy is entirely probable. Morning is the best time to focus on protection, because it's like putting a big coat on before you go out. This stops people draining your energy without them even knowing they are doing so.

I'll explain how I protect and ground myself then you can use the same or adapt to better suit yourself. Granny-May taught me the way, and I have not changed or adapted it, but you may want to do so depending upon your own beliefs or preferences. But this way has served me well for more years than I dare to mention.

There will be days when you forget, or the demands of life get in the way, but you will soon find it becomes part of your morning routine: Wash, Clean teeth, Protection and Grounding. It's all about setting an intention with belief and conviction. So I do mine standing and in my bedroom where I will, probably, not get disturbed: This is my choice. Some have an individual or sacred space; this is their choice. So I close my eyes, relax, and imagine a pure white light descending from the universe and totally enveloping me right down to the ground, and nothing will penetrate this bubble of pure white light (I often imagine negative words or situations after that bouncing off the bubble of white light), totally protected. Then I envision roots coming out of the soles of my feet and anchoring me firmly to the earth. I then ask for all negative energy to be drained away into the ground. I ask my Guides and Spirit family to protect me and keep me safe throughout this day and finish with a prayer of gratitude: I quite like the image of 'the Man with the beard', so I thank Him, you may have another, and that's fine too.

Now we all have our way. The key here is to protect and ground yourself so providing you set the intention, put yourself in a bubble of light and anchor yourself to the ground you will be just fine. I am sure your protection and grounding ritual will grow but for now, keep it simple.

Set intention (Belief and conviction)

A bubble of light (Protection)

Roots into the ground (Grounding)

As mentioned earlier I cannot emphasise the importance of protection and grounding especially if you are deciding to work with the general public. Granny-May always used to say, as above, as below, because Spirit retains their character and personality. And not all come from a loving place and work with love and light, do your protection and grounding, and you will be just fine. If you decide to venture to the dark side, you do this at your peril and don't come running to me when it all goes wrong as I'll be running in the opposite direction.

Spirit Guides:

This is a subject that pages and pages could be written about and nothing would match your own experiences. All you need in the beginning is your 'Gatekeeper Guide', and your team will grow and develop over time. Some guides stay with you all your life while others come and go throughout your development: Development Guides. I have had guides come through for a specific reading then never heard from them again. Your 'Gatekeeper Guide' is the Guide that's been with you since the day of your birth and you've probably met before you even entered the fetus for a briefing and pre-birth pep-talk. Guides are light-beings from a higher vibration who chooses to work with you from the day you are born. They are there to guide and protect you and develop your spiritual growth.

A high percentage of people never acknowledge their 'Gatekeeper Guide' and live their life only in the physical world. Therefore not developing and advancing spiritually and leaving 'Earth School' without any Spiritual Progression; you may say failing their 'O' levels in Spiritual Enlightenment. Remember when we die the only thing we can take home with us is our thoughts, so everything we gather physical is worthless: The rich man is the one who has advanced spiritually. The spirit world is nothing like here! The Soul has no gender. We enter the fetus as a sexless Soul and become whatever the body type is – Male or Female and develop physically and mentally according to our body type. We on earth need male and female to guarantee the continuation of the species, but in the Spirit world, we are that, Spirit energy.

We are all placed in 'Earth School' to learn a lesson and your 'Gatekeeper guide' accompanies you through your learning period but cannot change the outcome of your own decisions: Free will is yours! Spending time with your 'Gatekeeper Guide' can help you make better intuitive decisions but the final decision is always yours to make:

That's called free will and learning from your mistakes. When we go home to the Spirit world we continue to grow and develop spirituality; not knowing where our next journey will be: Exciting! Maybe, we spend time on other planets, in different bodies, to experience different things. Here's a thought for you to mull-over; What if aliens are just like us in different body types? Well, cars come in all shapes, sizes, colours and designs; what if bodies do too? I think that our solar system is just a pinhead of what, and indeed who, is out there: In the great plan of all things, maybe, this is something we are never meant to know? This world is by no means an accident. It is a carefully designed, self-sufficient, place to nurture earthly beings. Although we are destroying it through nothing more than human greed: Taking everything out and putting nothing back! When someone says to me they are sceptic and when your dead your dead. I reply that I feel this is not a very intelligent statement. Even the greatest minds alive have not established what comes after space. The only word they use is infinity. But to me, this word means nothing more than we don't know! It has always been obvious to me that there is more to life's great puzzle because of the humanly baffling intelligence that nature holds. For example, how does a Snowdrop know to pop its head up in February? Why does it not come up in 'flaming' June when it's warm? Why do Blackberry's fruit in August and not April? Why does the sea stop at the beach every-time? And the miracle of the human body's ability to heal. Even Doctors are still amazed at how after a laceration the wound heals perfectly. And how does a complex human body remain so resilient?

Now you've got me going. Back to the job in hand. Guides act as a link between you and the Spirit World: So ask and it will be given.

Your 'Gatekeeper Guide' will keep negative energies away and build better communication links with Spirits that want to communicate. People often ask me why so many Guides are Native American Indians, Chinese Medical Practitioners, Buddhist Monks? One answer is that all these have lived and worked in cultures and places of higher spirituality. But I feel that often Guides show themselves in a way most comfortable to you. As stated earlier the Soul is gender-less, but you may feel more comfortable with a male Guide than a women Guide; So that is what you get. You, yourself may have an interest in Red Indians, so your Guide may be seen by you as a great Indian Chief. It doesn't matter whether your 'Gatekeeper Guide' is the Great Geronimo, Buffalo Bill or Bill from Barnsley, they have been carefully chosen as your principal teachers. To help and control all your work on a spiritual level. Provide a point of contact, a figure to relate to, and a focal point to attune to. Your 'Gatekeeper Guide' will have an identity that feels right for you, a name that resonates with you and the ability to protect and work with you to develop your spiritual growth which continues in the Spirit world and each incarnation after that. Over time they can morph appearances but will always remain the same Soul. Your 'Gatekeeper Guide' will never free you from the responsibilities of making the wrong decisions in your life. Decision making is the principal part of learning and your earthly education; the fundamental reason for being here. You will always be responsible for your own decisions and always allowed the final say!

So let's meet your 'Gatekeeper Guide'. But we must first create a place of meeting, and we call this place your 'Heartspace' and your 'Psychic Workshop'.

> 'I am learning to sit in myself – To truly
> sit in my Heartspace.'

'Heartspace' is an Inner-Sanctum, first created by imagination, where Body, Mind, Soul and Spirit connect. A place where you go to be fully present and rooted in your essence. Where a direct line of communication is opened to the subconscious mind and the place of all Spirit communication: A place where everything is possible and nothing is impossible. A place where real change can take place at the source of all our thoughts: The subconscious mind. 'Heartspace' is a place where you can meet and communicate with your Spirit family to strengthen those all important links to the Spirit world and the emphasis on these relationships cannot be overstated. So let us meet this all-important 'Gatekeeper Guide'.

First, find somewhere to sit where you will not be disturbed for the duration of this exercise. Straight back and feet planted firmly on the floor. Close your eyes and relax (Imagination now becomes the language of choice as we close down the outside physical world for a short while and open up the world within). I want you to imagine you are now stood in-front of a door. It doesn't matter what types of entry it is. Just a door. Is it an old door with bolts and rivets or maybe your front door? In a moment I will ask you to open the door and step through into your 'Heartspace'. It could be a soft sandy beach. An enchanted forest. An exotic garden. Or just a simple meadow dotted with wildflowers and a steady flowing stream. This is your place, a safe place. So now I want you to open the door and step through. Explore this place. Take your time. Don't rush. You have all the time in the world. As you explore this beautiful place, I would like you now to find somewhere to sit. Maybe there is an up-turned log or a park bench. But find somewhere to sit. As you sit, I want you to call upon your 'Gatekeeper Guide'. Imagine your 'Gatekeeper Guide' walking out from behind a big tree or rock. Appearing from round a corner or just manifesting in front of you. Then standing in-front of you or sitting next to you. Now really take a good look at your 'Gatekeeper Guide'. Is your Guide male or female. Young or old. What's the colour of his/her skin. What's the colour of his/her Hair: Is it long or short; straight or curly. Do they have facial hair: A Beard maybe or moustache. Clothes: What period are your Guides clothes from and what do they tell you about him/her. Is your Guide tall or short, stocky or thin? The more information you can gather the better you become to know your Guide. Record all you see in your mind (After the exercise is complete record all your observations in a journal or if you are an arty person then draw or paint your guide). Now ask your guide for a name. Take the first name that comes into your mind. You can even ask if your Guide has a message for you or any information he/she can pass onto you that may help you in your development. Be brave! Now say good-bye to your Guide and find the door you first came through. Go back through the door and be sure to close the door behind you. Then when you are ready slowly open your eyes and return to the here and now.

So how did that go? Remember, development takes time. You may have only got a little this time, or you may have got a lot. Either way, it is not a competition, and with dedication, time and practice you will create your success. So don't demand and be too hard on yourself. You will get there! 'Heartspace' is a place where you can also work on yourself: Your psychic workshop. We can never change ourselves with anything physical. Only by changing our thoughts and thinking can real change take place: Think right, feel right. Thoughts become things, and all things once started as a thought. So the way we think is vital to what we create within our subconscious mind as often its not the outside world that causes us problems but the world we create with our minds: The perspective world. Imagination is the language of the subconscious mind we can, therefore, change the perspective world within to help with our personal growth and development. Try by seeing old memory's on a cinema screen in your 'Heartspace' and how you once reacted to them. Then return the same memory but see a different outcome with the all important different reaction. You will be amazed by just a little work the difference you will see in yourself in a short space of time. The possibilities are endless. I hope you are still excited?

So let me remind you how important your imagination is. Imagination to some is not seeing pictures but being aware of the images. For others, it's like a trip to the movies. You will find your way of using your imagination.

We have to use what we have been given. We all use imagination in the recall of information from memory. If I was to say to you, what's the colour of your front door? You would first think, recall by imagination, then say the colour. Some would see a white door: Some would have a knowing, and either way works perfectly well. Imagination is a place where Spirit connect with your mind through thoughts. Imagination works equally well with eyes open or closed; closed eyes just aid concentration by removing unnecessary distractions. People who often find themselves daydreaming access their creativity. But that doesn't mean that the more logical, here and now person can't learn to access their imagination just as well, although with a bit more time and practice. We can't all be the stereotype 'Walter Mitty's' of the world: Not sure if that would be a good thing after seeing the film. You can now use 'Heartspace' or your 'Psychic Workshop' for development work from getting to know your guides better to connecting with your Spirit family.

So now before we move on to opening up, I want to take a little time to talk about your Spirit family. Your Spirit family consists of family members and loved ones who have passed over to the Spirit world who will help you with your Spiritual work and growth: Usually having human connections and part of your Soul Group. But think: Is everyone on earth part of our Soul Group with other planets housing other Soul Groups or do different Soul Groups mix with ours? Lots of questions still to be answered but always look for the bigger picture and do not become restricted to narrow mindedness!

My Grandmother, Grandfather, Mother and Father often help me with readings, assisting my 'Gatekeeper Guide' to make sure the right people come through for the attending sitter. One way I get people through is I imagine my Granny-May being in charge of a lift from the Spirit World to my reading room. She will call people to step into the elevator for the attending sitter and bring them down. They will then take their position by the Sitter. I have a rule if its mother's side they stand to the right and if its dads side to the left. Others, for example, friends and acquaintances stand a little way from the sitter. This is just my way, and I am sure you will come up with your own set of rules.

Remember your team will build over time and the right Guides will appear at the right time. Also, Animal Spirit Guides will often show themselves to you and can become a significant part of your team as lots of sitters have lost pets, and your Animal Guides will best bring them through. I had a lady come for a reading, and I told her I had a Yorkshire terrier around my feet and it said to me that it had nothing to go back for. To her this was the best thing that could have happened with her saying, he won't, he was my baby. But for now let's keep it simple, one step at a time. Remember Spirit know what you are trying to do and will assist you all they can. Spirit has a funny way of getting you to do what they want you to do. They have got you this far, so they are not going to abandon you now: Worry not my dear.

There is always a debate as to whether we should open up, then close down or stay open. My view is that I prefer to open up and close down because it lets Spirit know when I'm working and when I'm not. I am sensitive, and spirit will pass on messages throughout the day. Every opportunity possible to talk (and want to help) to their loved ones: Who wouldn't. So I prefer to open up and close down, though if a message is essential and I am closed down my Guides will allow them through, and I don't mind that at all. But we mediums need our rest and grounding time, so that's my reason for opening and closing, but you may be different: Let's see, shall we? So before I start my Spiritual work, bearing in mind I have done my protection and grounding that morning, I will stand and plant my feet firmly on the floor in a bubble of beautiful white light, imagining roots growing from my feet going deep into the ground and just have a moment or two to calm and quieten the mind. Then I say my opening prayer.

'I now call upon my highest and most divine Guides; Spirit Guides, Helpers, Inspirers and Protectors to now assist me connecting with the Spirit world safely. I ask for only information and guidance that is loving and purposeful – Amen'

I then call upon my Guides to draw close to me as well as my Spirit family to make the information I receive concise, clear and understandable. I then flick my switch to Spiritual Ida and open my chakras. I will explain it.

Chakras are a receptor and play an essential part in your psychic / mediumship awareness. We have seven main chakras starting at the crown and finishing at the base of our spine. So when we work spiritually we open up our chakras and when our work is done we close them down. I see six of my chakras as rose buds and the brow chakra (Situated between your eye brows and often referred to as the third eye chakra) I see as a purple eye. When I open my chakras, I start at the base and work up to the crown seeing the rose buds bursting open and pulsing with energy in their relevant, vibrant colours. Upon opening my brow chakra, or third eye chakra, I know this chakra as a purple eye-opening, and I always give it a few blinks just like we do on a morning after a good nights sleep. Upon closing, I do the reverse. That's starting by closing the crown chakra, then closing the third eye chakra, then the rest of the chakras right down to the base. Below I have listed the seven main chakras and their positions and colours, but there are many books for further reference.

Crown – White

Brow or third eye – Purple

Throat – Blue

Heart – Green

Solar Plexus – Yellow

Sacral – Orange

Base – Red

Now we are open we are ready for work. Upon closing we must remember to thank Spirit, and be grateful for allowing us to work with them: Remember the words Respect and Gratitude. I feel very privileged that Spirit will enable me to work with them and I know they can stop it whenever they want. I always thank my Guides and Spirit family and ask that they watch over me and the world. You will find your way, and this will become second nature.

Right, let's now do another exercise. Ask a friend to place a photograph of one of their family members (or maybe even a pet, adjusting the questioning to suit), someone you have not met and know nothing about who has passed to the Spirit World, into a sealed down envelope. Then sitting at a table place your hand on the envelope containing the photograph and answer these questions. The key here is to say the first thing that comes into your head and TRUST what you get is RIGHT. Document the exercise in your journal so you can see your progression the next time you do it.

Ask: Is this male or female?

Ask: What job did they do?

Ask: What did they look like – Hair Colour, etc.?

Ask: Were they married or single?

Ask: Did they have children – If so how many?

Ask: What were their interests or hobbies?

Ask: What was their name? (Don't be too hard on yourself with this one. Just try).

Ask: How old were they when they passed?

Ask: What did they pass with – Illness etc.?

Feel free to ask your questions and always trust the answers you get; never consciously analyse them and once you have finished your questioning open the envelope. Bet you're nervous now! But you needn't be as you are only learning and the one thing I can promise is that even after years of practice you will never get it right all of the time. I don't! Its easy to misinterpret what Spirit are trying to show us. I once asked another medium when I was starting how she handled the No's she sometimes received. She said she never got No's. And I can now say in all confidence that if she had been Pinocchio, she would have taken my sitting room window out. No's are amazing. Never be frightened of a No.

At times all mediums get it wrong as Spirit messages can be so very subtle. Often we will misinterpret something due to nothing more than the messages are not meant for us to understand, and it's not our job to understand, only deliver. Never assume and keep intelligent analysis out of it. I often say to my sitter. This means nothing to me, so I hope you understand: And mostly they do. If you become frightened of getting it wrong or fail to trust what you get you may hold something back that means the world to your sitter and the reason they are here. So as I always say, I will give you everything I get, and it's then up to you, the sitter, to make sense of it.

I hold nothing back, I trust my Guides implicitly, and all the No's make all the Yes's so much more amazing. Yes, even I after all my years can still be amazed at the evidence Spirit give. You see my dear every reading is different. This job is not like a production line where everything is the same day in and day out. If that's what you want: It's a career at Ben Shaws for you (Local Huddersfield soft drinks manufacturers) on the production line. Reading is exciting and unpredictable, and before any reading, I have nothing until the sitter sits in front of me then we're off. It will never change.

All you have to do is place your 'TRUST' in your Guides; they will never let you down. Some weeks I have done up to thirty-five / forty readings, and I never think about them until I hear the knock on the door. It's too late then to run for the hills. I think that nerves are a good thing and when we stop feeling them maybe, that's the time to give up. Complacent is something I have never become, or taken anything spiritual for granted, because I am only working for Spirit and as mentioned earlier they can stop you if they feel you are abusing your privilege: Remember 'RESPECT' and 'GRATITUDE', and trust me you will never become bigger or better than Spirit! That's why I always say, never do it for the money. If you do it like me for the passion, the money will follow. They will always make sure you have enough and as I say enough is quite sufficient for me. Spirit is an excellent company to work for because they always look after their staff: Maybe you'll not become a regular shopper at Marks & Spencers, but you will always have enough for Woolworth's.

So how have you done? Did you here your inner-voice? Did you see images? Did you feel something? Or did you know? However, you've done you've tried, and like all things with practice, you will get better. So well done you! If your friend can stay a while then let me show you what else you can practice together.

But before we start let me explain the difference between a psychic, a medium and a clairvoyant, as this is something I am often asked. Psychics are said to obtain their information by intuitively reading energies (Auras, etc.), often using a mix of tools (Tarot Cards, Crystals, Colours, Etc) whereas mediums communicate directly with Spirit; that's people who have passed over to the Spirit world or Spirit Guides. Mediums also read energies, and they too can use various tools (Psychometry, Tarot Cards, Oracle cards, Etc) but they get their information directly from Spirit and Spirit Guides.

As a Medium, I work with Spirit. My cards tell me nothing until Spirit tell me what a particular card means for the attending sitter. So one card could have a different meaning for a hundred different people. I also use my psychic abilities, for example, when the sitter's aura merges with mine. That is the reason why I like to work on a one to one basis as I find this works best for me, although for whatever reasons some sitters auras will retract and that makes psychic reading much more difficult; but you will find your way and what works best for you. Trust me, its not all text book stuff in the mediumship game, and that's why trial and error is essential in your early days of development: So you see you have to fail to be a success. I've been knocked down eight times and got up nine, actually probably more like a hundred times and got up a hundred and one, and I probably will get knocked down a few more times yet before I'm done, but one thing I can guarantee is that I will always keep getting back up – I've told my family that when I pass they'd better nail the coffin lid down well! Now, where was I. A psychic is not always classed as a medium, but mediums are usually classed as psychic… Confused yet? Readers typically follow a path that they feel is more dominant and shows most strength within the individual. A clairvoyant (Clairvoyance – Clear seeing) receive their information visually. The titles can all be interchangeable depending on the development of the person. With development things do change, but I do feel it's just we become more aware. I think that even people who class themselves as just psychic receive information from Spirit its just that at this moment in time they are not mindful of Spirit around them. Often they will call it intuition, but are intuition and gut feeling Spirit communication? So the difference between Psychic and medium is a very grey area, so all I will say is that the Medium is aware of Spirit communication, but the psychic may be unaware of how much of their information is indeed from Spirit and Spirit Guides. And that does make sense. Doesn't it? Others may receive information by one or all the clairs… Clairaudience (Clear Hearing), Clairsentience (Clear Feeling), Claircogizance (Clear Knowing), Clairgustance (Clear Tasting). You see things change when you develop awareness and that why it's not textbook stuff because we all build awareness differently. Sometimes there could be no more exact words said than, fly by the seat of your pants, because mediumship cannot be taught it has to be developed and development takes time and time is something that cannot be rushed or bought.

So is the Psychic a Medium that is unaware of Spirit? And in-fact is all information received transmitted from our Spirit Guides and Spirit family to the exchange within the subconscious mind and made available in some logical way by the inner-voice of the mind through one of the "clairs". I think there is still a lot we don't know so to keep things simple take the information received in whatever way it is given to you and TRUST that what you have been given is right. And pass it on. Do we need the word Psychic? Are we all Spiritual Mediums working with our Spiritual Team? I doubt very much that without Spirit and Spirit Guides we would receive or understand little if any information, have any gut feelings or even any intuition.

Clair's, well they are just the ear piece to the Spiritual phone. Glad that bits over!

So back to your friend. By the way I hope you have given them a drink of tea and a biscuit? Ask your friend to imagine a number from one to ten. And send the number to your mind. Sit facing each-other. I want you to receive that number. Imagine a telephone line from your mind to theirs. Or see the number jumping from their mind to yours. Concentrate. Imagine the number. Then say the very first number that enters your mind. How did you do? Did you imagine the number? Did you hear the number? Did you feel the number or know the number? Remember all the information comes into your subconscious mind: Your Spiritual exchange centre. If you were spot on then well done you. If you were not then maybe you haven't yet cracked your code of Spirit communication: Patience. You can do this exercise with various things, words, fruit, colours. Just have fun!

Now it's going to get exciting because we are nearly ready to embark on our first reading; but first an 'err on the side of caution' warning! When we work as a medium not only are we seen as a reader by the sitter but often their therapist. Whatever is said to you as a medium is said in total confidence and must at all times be treated as such. This may sound obvious but often when we are with a bunch of friends who are quite open with each other and the wine is flowing we can often, unintentionally, let our mouth run away with us and something trivial or funny to you could be immensely embarrassing or confidential to your sitter. You never know who knows who and even who is listening in to your conversation. The general rule of any professional is: What's said in a reading stays in the reading. Once trust is broken others will see you as despicable. Don't let careless words ruin your reputation! Also, you will need insurance and a disclaimer. The protection should be public liability and indemnity as you cannot be insured for what you say only if your sitter falls or trips. That is what you are protected for. The disclaimer covers you by stating that the reading is for entertainment purposes only and your actions and responses to the reading are your responsibility: Remember, some are looking for a fast buck!

So let's now talk a little about tools. Some mediums who call themselves 'natural mediums' shun cards as gimmicks. Well, I have used my cards from day one, and I would feel lost without them. They are a great tool for interpretation, but as a medium, my advice is don't become a card reader. I have in the past seen many readers simply tell the sitter what the cards mean and even at one time from a book on their table. My cards mean nothing until Spirit tell me what the card means for the attending sitter. So one card could have a hundred different meanings for a hundred different sitters. As we go we learn the basics of tarot, that is unavoidable, but at this point don't worry about the meanings more what the card means at the time of the reading for that particular sitter – Let the cards speak! Spirit know you are just starting and will treat you as such and as with time you learn some of the cards they will use this to their advantage: Remember they will always know where you are in your development and your present capabilities and will treat you accordingly. For all the years I have been reading I am no expert on the tarot, and probably never will be, and neither do you need to be. But cards are a helpful tool, and a tool is what they are. I call my cards Spiritual cards, and not tarot cards, even though they were purchased as such. Some people use crystals, colours, ruins. It doesn't matter as long as you say what's in your head and not what's written in a book: There is no room for conscious logic in Spirit communication. Tools help keep focus and another line of communication: Tools of interpretation.

When we first start reading it is always best to start with someone we don't know because as the saying goes 'a little information is dangerous'. If we know the slightest thing about our sitter, it can cause conflict between what we receive subconsciously and what we feel is logic. When someone sits with me, I never chat before the reading. I do the reading then there is plenty of time to talk after that. Family and friends never make good sitters because we know too much about them and that takes away useful validation, and often we fail by trying too hard: Trying to achieve the 'wow' factor. But as mentioned before don't be too hard on yourself at the beginning, Doris Stokes had to start somewhere! And TRUST, TRUST, TRUST what you get and ALWAYS give what you get and NEVER be afraid of a no… No's are GREAT!

Someone once said to me that the best way to learn is by booking a reading and if it all goes wrong have a cry then book another because you will learn far more with it all going wrong than you ever will with it all going right. Good advice, I think.

So now let me show you my way; so the sitter is sat in-front of me. I have already opened up, protected and grounded myself. I have asked my Guides to draw close to me and asked my Spirit family for their help. Just for a moment I sit quietly and raise my awareness of Spirit. Sometimes listening to a piece of music or a short meditation before the sitter arrives helps to achieve this. With practice raising your consciousness will be like switching on a light. I first tell the sitter how 'I' work. I tell them everything I give comes from Spirit: Their Guides and mine, and our Spiritual families. That the information I receive means nothing to me, so I need a yes, no or maybe. That a reading is a three-way communication between the sitter, myself and Spirit, then I will hand them the cards and ask them to shuffle the pack while thinking about their Spirit family and how they want their life to be, or not. In a reading I would never ask a question, always tell the sitter, never asking. Questions are seen as fishing and something that damages effective validation. I then tell them to take their time shuffling and when they are ready hand the pack back. I then fan the cards and ask them to pick thirteen: Remember this is my way and you will find yours. Once they have given me the thirteen, I spread them in three rows of four and one at the top. I look at the cards and start reading. I cannot tell you anything about the reading as nothing is in my mind until I start. It is no good worrying about a reading beforehand because most often nothing is received until the start of a reading and with time this does not change. And as I always say what's the worst that can happen if you receive nothing is you don't charge the client. There will be times when you have to stop a reading, but to my mind, this is a good thing and by not charging you retain your credibility. Once another medium

I was telling that I had to stop a reading said, couldn't you just have rambled on about something or other to finish the reading and get your money. Trust me it is not worth it and will do you more harm than good. I work by the three no's rule. If I get three no's at the beginning of a reading, I stop the reading, and say that I am not connecting for some reason and don't charge the sitter. This has always stood me in good stead and even got me more work due to being honest with my sitters. Some readers will tell you they have never stopped a reading. Don't believe them. We all have, and you will too. Remember a reading is a three-way effort or conversation and if one of the three is not playing their full part then there is only one thing you can do, and that is to stop the reading before making a fool of yourself – for whatever the reason is.

A reading has no set time. Some readings can be fifteen minutes while others can be an hour. My Guides will stop the reading when the sitter's needs have been given, and yours will too. But at first keep it simple: Your Guides will know you have your L plates on! People often attend a reading to hopefully be connected with a loved-one as well as receiving guidance from their Guides and Spirit family, or a more specific reason. I never ask the reason for the reading, I say if I miss something we can discuss it at the end. We can never bring anybody back and make them communicate. We can never guarantee a specific Spirit will come through. All we can do is try for the sitter. With time and practice communication with Spirit will become more explicit, but I cannot give anymore guarantee than you can and never will be able to. Spirit link with your mind, and communicate in various ways, and only by practice will you learn this what now seems a foreign language. I, being me, always add humour to my readings, and this is of benefit when dealing with sad and upsetting situations. I like people to leave feeling a little better than when they first came, but don't allow this to create an avoidance of certain subjects. Spirit will never give you anything they don't want your sitter to know but remember it's all in the delivery. You are a sensitive so deliver how you would want to receive, and you will not go wrong. This world is not all buttercups and daisies, and if Spirit tells you something then they want it passing on, and they trust you will do it with tact and decorum. They will never tell you when a person will die, but they may say if that person is, for example, abusing alcohol, if you don't change your drinking habits you may well walk in front of a bus!

Remember when giving a message…Contact / Link – Validation of Evidence and Message – Thank Spirit. Sometimes Spirit only want us to know they are alright and give us a hug, whereas other times its one of guidance and counsel: Give what you get!

'I have never once had Spirit say they are unhappy at home, in the spirit world, it's their family and friends down here they worry about!'

After I have ended the reading, we chat a while maybe over a cup of tea and a biscuit, and answer any questions or concerns the sitter may have. After the sitter has left I close down and rejoin life. A reading is a guidance. You're not a fortune teller. We all start life at 'A' and finish at 'B' and not always take the most direct route. Spirit try to keep you on the motorway of life when you want to make the twists and turns of the country lanes, but remember we all have free will: Often to our detriment, but always to our learning!

> 'We accumulate our wisdom and
> knowledge through experience.'

HERE IS AN EXAMPLE OF A READING WHICH CAUSED PROBLEMS:
DEAL WITH THE SITUATION SWIFTLY AND WITH CLARITY:

A gentleman came for a reading admitting he was a sceptic: I often wonder how people get through life thinking 'once you're dead you're dead'. Two of his friends had both been before, and they had had beautiful readings so he thought he would come and let me try to convince him of life after death. More probably he wanted to prove to his friends that mediumship is all nonsense and that we mediums are nothing more than a bunch of charlatans.

During the reading, I explained there would be a new opportunity for him in February. He instantly and sharply replied: NO! I asked him how did he know there would be no opportunity for him in February? Three No's later: And he's out of the door! You see he did not see any further than the end of his nose. A reading is a guidance and Spirit only want to make us aware of opportunities that will advance us further along our Spiritual path. This gentleman has a job, and an excellent job may I say, but cannot see past that job. He will probably retire in that job and die without any further learning or advancement because of nothing more than his lateral thinking and closed mind: What a waste of a life... And reading.

But there is nothing you or I can do about this situation. The best way is to stop the reading and send him and others like him on their way because it will be like running into a brick wall: A pointless exercise. If I could say, 'I have your mother here, she says that you put your dirty underpants back on today and didn't even turn them inside out.' He may have been impressed. One-day that may happen, but not with a closed mind I fear.

THE REVERSE ALSO HAPPENED:

A young lady came for a reading. She listened intently throughout the reading to everything I told her. At the end she said that not much made sense right now but let us see. Twelve months later she returned and said that it all makes perfect sense now. And she brought three of her friends for readings too. You see, she was open-minded, and gave the messages Spirit sent her time to happen. Remember free will, you do have a choice, but I always trust Spirit, and they have never let me down: So, be guided by the inner voice of Spirit and Trust!

"I am no better than you; I have just had more practice"
– Ida Pimm.

Now then how are we doing my dear? Great I hope. Granny-May showed me a way of bringing Spirit through that often helps at the beginning of development, and you can try this way now as an exercise. Get your friend (Not insinuating in any way that you only have the one) and ask them to sit facing you. Imagine a person stood behind them. Now focus on this person and not the sitter and describe the person to the sitter. Pass on all the information to the sitter; your friend. Give all you can and even ask if there is a message for your friend. Remember don't be too hard on yourself as Spirit can pass on images and symbols much more natural than words but as yet you are not fully competent with the language so you will probably miss something that with time will become so prominent. Be brave; give everything – TRUST! Now ask your friend if there is anything they can take. Remember the most insignificant piece of information to you could be the most significant and touching to your friend. However you have done you have tried, and I cannot overemphasise the importance of PRACTICE MAKES PERFECT in your Spiritual development and time; you cannot rush time. Now it's all down to you. Mediumship cannot be taught; it has to be developed. You have all the instruction you need. The seed has been germinated now let it grow. Practice all you can. Read for as many people as you can. Don't be afraid, Ida knows you can do it! You see it is not as difficult as you think, it's a natural part of us that has been forgotten not lost. It is still there you have to learn to trust the intangible and stop relying on the tangible as most people do! A friend of mine, a farmer, once said that he understood things he could see, a jar of nails is a jar of nails, but will never understand what I do: He needs to change his way of thinking, I think.

As we develop, it is often a natural progression to enter the world of Spiritual Healing. That's allowing the energy of Spirit to flow through you in a way that rejuvenates others. Most often a Spiritual Healer is a wounded healer and from their own personal experiences make the best candidates to heal others. The Spiritual aspect refers to Spiritual energy working at a deep level on our Spiritual being: We all need a Spiritual hug from time to time and maybe reconnect for a little while to our own Soul Groups and Spirit families when ailing or going through a tough time – Emotional or physical. The preparation for Healing is the same as for a reading. In-fact by placing your hands on another after PROTECTION, GROUNDING and OPENING the benefits can be truly amazing. Sometimes we think that if something is too simple, it will not work and that by overcomplicating what was first given in its most simplistic form we can make it work better: Often we are wrong.

We are only the conductor for this energy so by keeping the conductor pure we pass on undistorted energy to the receptor. So I believe concerning Spiritual Healing the simpler, the better. As mentioned earlier often we make things overcomplicated and over protracted to justify their worth. If a course of learning has a module or session value, then modules or sessions could be added to increase the monetary value consequently polluting its purity at the source. So my advice is to keep it simple and let Spirit guide you. I feel that the best way of learning is by doing, so be brave and as the old saying goes 'fake it till you make it,' as this statement holds a lot of truth: Don't tell your sitters you are just starting out; you are a medium! Because without practice we achieve nothing: A surgeon at some time has to make his first cut.

I feel that out of all the varieties of mediumship, Spiritual Healing is the least appreciated and the least attractive to the potential medium. All mediums can act as a healer, and there is nothing more rewarding than to see someone healed whether on an emotional level or physical. All that is needed by the medium is to call on their Guides and Spirit Family. They will take care of the rest. It is often beneficial for the Healer to place their hands, after asking permission from the recipient, on or near the place that requires healing. Spiritual Healing has always worked best for me standing behind or in front of the recipient and allowing my hands to rest lightly on their shoulders. And always be prepared for tears, tears are good. We are like a bottle of champagne, and sometimes we need the cork to pop and release the bubbles: Tears. Often the procedure is straightforward but the results are dramatic, and you will be amazed at the difference YOU can make to the lives of others!

When I am healing I work through my Spirit Doctors, Healing Guides, Spirit Guides and Spirit family: My team. I create a link, a channel, allowing extraordinary healing to take place. I often use psychic surgery, telling the recipient what my team are doing. The simple touch of another human produces incredible healing effects, so whatever you attempt Spirit will help you achieve something beautiful for your fellow man. You may want to start by holding another person's hand and allow Spirit to do the rest, and don't be surprised what this may achieve. Because Spirit contact and communication is Mind to Mind then maybe we need Spirit to trigger the healing from their mind to ours. Ah, there is so much we don't know, but often the old ways are still the best – And their is nothing older than Spiritual Healing!

When we work with Spirit, or indeed any of the healing arts, we must not neglect ourselves and always leave time for self-healing and personal growth and development. By learning about ourselves and working on ourselves, we create a better understanding of our fellow man and rid our minds of accumulated clutter and junk, becoming that clearer channel when we connect to Spirit. Our minds become so cluttered; it's like having a hundred people on the phone at once. Past Life Regression, Hypnotherapy are all excellent ways of expanding our knowledge about ourselves and who we are: Clearing the clutter. Some of you may want to explore Physical mediumship with all its ectoplasm and séance trumpets. Physical mediumship was very popular in the Victorian era but its interest wained, hopefully, to return at a later date. This type of mediumship is not for me but maybe for you? You may want to learn about apports or Spirit rescue? But remember, at first, keep it simple. You see mediums are just ordinary people, with regular jobs who choose to work for Spirit and whatever you feel drawn to will work best for you. Mental mediumship suits me because I like the counselling and the helping of people approach to my Spiritual work, but we are not all the same, so you choose!

So all you need to remember now is, TRUST, RESPECT & GRATITUDE and PRACTICE… PRACTICE…

PRACTICE. I presume that by the time you are reading these words I shall be on the other side of life, but all you need to do is enter your 'Heartspace' and shout Ida, and I shall be there ready to work with you: God Bless.

Ida Pimm

And a final word from John Richardson:

You should by now realise that becoming a medium, spiritual healer/therapist, is as much about changing yourself as it is about connecting to Spirit: And at a subconscious level. The subconscious mind holds a record of everything you have ever seen and done. It accumulates information about daily life experience. Not all is to our advantage. Soon the mind contains many emotional toxins or mind junk, blocking what would otherwise be an evident channel to Spirit.

One reason why when we are young we are naturally connected to Spirit, is, our mind junk or emotional toxins are limited. Working on ourselves is an essential factor of reconnecting our Natural Inborn Abilities at a subconscious level.

If you are struggling to connect to Spirit when reading for clients, or in healings, then these could be the most important words you will ever read, because before you can heal others you have first to heal yourself.

Most psychics, mediums, healers and therapists have all walked challenging paths. You are reminded; many issues are felt and displayed as emotional, anxiety and nervous disorders. Problems may also manifest as fears, phobias and panic attacks, plus many other variations of neurotic symptoms. Although not always admitted by the medium, the issues create blocks, obstacles and avoidance's that hinder progression on both a personal and professional level. Symptoms that appear without any organic reason for their existence often have their roots planted firmly in past and previous lives. Therefore, reader, healer or therapist, sometimes associate with clients problems creating avoidances that all too often hinder a clients progression: And their own.

Regression Therapy is a Self-Exploratory Therapy Based Technique used to bring about the release of negative trapped emotions: Detaching active emotions from memories; triggered by association. They could be frequent and reoccurring neurotic symptoms, both mental and physical. The issues create blocks, obstacles and avoidance's commonly experienced amongst readers, healers and therapists alike.

Regression Therapy provides healing through understanding. Using advanced and innovated regression techniques 'The Regressor' will return the person to a 'life' or 'memory' most relevant to their issue. Providing the healing necessary to alleviate all unwanted symptoms. After this reading, healing and therapy can be conducted free of blocks and obstacles that previously created hindrance and avoidance.

HypnoAnalysis (Present Life Regression) or Past Life Regression Therapy (Past Life Regression) is recommended for all practising psychics, mediums and therapists, to clear the mind of its, mainly unavoidable, juvenile faulty programming which in-turn creates the root cause of many present-day, presenting symptoms. Note: Most neurotic symptoms are formed in present life and are in need of HypnoAnalysis. For more information visit the website or call: 07800584077

At the beginning of this book Ida mentioned Arthur's grandson who was to be born, well, I am that grandson. I feel I learnt from the best, both Hypnosis and Spiritualism, and in my work I have blended the two very successfully. Other teachers have helped form the person I have now become, and a special thank you to one, Mr Simon Goodfellow, but it was aunt Ida and my grandfather that set the foundations and set the proverbial wheels in motion. The words in this book that aunt Ida left behind have now become the teachings of Psychic and Mediumship Development for the National Association Of Holistic Analytical Hypnotherapists: Blending Hypnosis with Spirituality. More information can be found at www.feelbetterfast.co.uk and www.john-richardson.co.uk and the many courses the Association now runs. And all this stems from these two very special people: Ida Pimm and J. Arthur Laundon.

John Richardson – Owner/Founder of The Feel
Better Fast Clinic and Principal/Teacher of The National
Association Of Holistic Analytical Hypnotherapists.
Psychic Spiritual Medium

COURSES AVAILABLE

PSYCHIC & MEDIUMSHIP DEVELOPMENT:

The course teaches the three levels of Psychic and Mediumship Development based on the teachings of Ida Pimm: Includes Spiritual Counselling and Healing over three weekends:

Weekend 1 – Level 1 – Inception
Weekend 2 – Level 2 – Transition
Weekend 3 – Level 3 – Graduate

On completion of all three levels the 'Student' will receive a 'Certificate of Competence' accredited and supported by The National Association Of Holistic Analytical Hypnotherapists. (This course complements Holistic Analytical Hypnotherapy: Blending Hypnosis with Spirituality)

PAST LIFE REGRESSION TRAINING:

- The Art of Past Life Regression Therapy for Qualified Hypnotherapists
- Reading Past Lives (Also)
- Connect and Work with your Animal Spirit Guides
- Soul 2 Soul™ Past Life Regression & Spiritual Connections

Other courses will become available: Check the website.

TRAIN AND BECOME A
HOLISTIC ANALYTICAL HYPNOTHERAPIST:

- HOLISTIC ANALYTICAL HYPNOTHERAPY
with The National Association
Of Holistic Analytical Hypnotherapists

All courses are accredited, supported and run by
The National Association Of Holistic Analytical
Hypnotherapists
Principal/Teacher Mr. John Richardson

NAHAH – Courses and Workshops are group Centered:
Private one to one tuition is also available.

Further information:
Visit: www.feelbetterfast.co.uk
Visit: www.john-richardson.co.uk
Telephone: 07800584077

Past Life Oracle Cards

by John Richardson

John Richardson is one of the Uk's leading authorities on Past Life Regression & Past Life Readings... These Cards were channeled by John with two fundamental purposes in mind: 1. To help the individual access and recall information from previous Past Lifetimes that will help them in their life and work today, therefore providing Healing through Understanding, and, 2. To provide the Professional Psychic Spiritual Medium with a further tool to allow a deeper insight as to how 'Past Life Influence' can affect 'Present Biographical Lives'.

'Listen to your Soul and let your Soul speak'
'See how the Past affects the Present and influences the Future'

For more information Visit: www.feelbetterfast.co.uk or Call: 07800584077

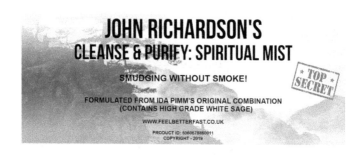

John Richardson's Cleanse & Purify: Spiritual Mist is formulated from his Great Aunt Ida's Original Combination containing High Grade White Sage and was passed on to him after her passing.

Traditionally Smudging involves the burning of White Sage to Cleanse and Purify the Soul and Space of Negative Energy... Creating Sacred Space.

Instead of Burning you can now Spray as some people find the smoke produced from burning White Sage can causes irratation... John Richardson's Cleanse & Purify: Spiritual Mist is Smudging without Smoke!

This time served 'Secret' formula of Great Aunt Ida's produces the same results without the smoke and with the added addition of a more fragrant aroma produced from this carefully selected blend of complementary essential oils than that of White Sage alone.

£15.00

For more information Visit: www.feelbetterfast.co.uk or Call: 07800584077

NOTES

NOTES

NOTES

NOTES